All From a Bottle

Anna Kunari

Illustrations by
Teri Sloat

HAMPTON·BROWN

One day, for Show-and-Tell, Rosa put a blue bottle near the edge of Mr. Hall's desk.

"When I went to Oregon last year," said Rosa, "I spent almost all of my time at the beach. One day, I found this bottle in the water. It turned out to be a very special bottle."

"Tell us about it," said Mr. Hall.

"You will never believe me," said Rosa.

"Try us," said Mr. Hall.

So Rosa began her story.

3

Rosa's Show-and-Tell Tale

I always like playing on the beach.
You can climb sand dunes. You can sit on
the edge of a rock and peer down into
the tide pools below. Best of all, the sea
brings interesting things up to the shore.
Sometimes you can find sea shells and
pretty rocks.

One day, I see this blue bottle
bobbing in the water. I almost walk past it,
but I see something in it. I yank out the
cork and use a small stick to fish out
a note. Does the note say, "HELP"? No.

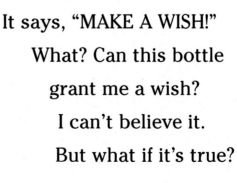

It says, "MAKE A WISH!"
What? Can this bottle
grant me a wish?
I can't believe it.
But what if it's true?

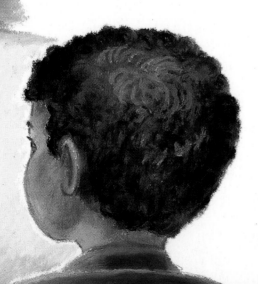

So I sit on the warm sand and think about all the things I could wish for. I could wish to be rich and important. I almost wish for that . . . but I don't.

I could wish to be invisible! I almost wish for that also . . . but I don't.

Then I think of a great wish. What if I could turn into all sorts of different shapes? I have always wanted to do that.

"Make me the best shape-shifter on earth!" I tell the bottle.

"You bet!" the bottle croaks.

BAM! I turn into a puddle!

"You tricked me!" I yell.

"Not at all," croaks the bottle.

"Water IS the best shape-shifter on earth!"

Should I believe that? Is water really
the best shape-shifter on all the earth?

As I think about it, the hot
sun beats down on me. Soon I am
so warm that I disappear into the air.

"You have just evaporated," laughs the bottle. "Now you are invisible! The heat of the sun has turned you into water vapor. Now you are a part of the air. Look out! Warm air always rises!"

The bottle is right. Up, up, up I climb, until I get cold and turn into a cloud. Soon a wind blows me high into the sky. Can you believe it? I am flying!

I slide over the edge of an airplane wing, then I swoop under a bird and tickle its tummy. The houses below me look as small as toys.

Then the sky
gets very cold. I turn
into snow and I float
down. Soon I fall in
a park, where a boy
makes me into a
snowball. He throws
the snowball at his
sister, and SPLAT!,
I fall into bits.

When the sun comes out, I melt back into water.
I flow into a gutter and then a creek, and then a river.
Off I go, faster and faster. Soon I hear a great roar.

"Yikes!" I yell. "That's
a waterfall! If I go over, I will
hit the rocks below!"

And over the falls I go,
all the way to the bottom.
I hit the rocks, BAM!

What a surprise!
It does not hurt at all! I just
turn into a mist, riding on
the wind. I climb into the sky
and turn into a cloud again,
sailing over the earth.

"Where to next?" calls
the wind.

"To the jungle!" I say
"It's time to get warm."

The wind blows and blows.
High over land and sea I fly,
over ships and whales.
At last, I turn into rain!

This time I fall through
a rainbow and turn red, orange,
yellow, green, blue, and purple.

Then down I go, much faster than snow, until I see a tall tree below with wide, green leaves.

SPLAT! I hit a leaf and hang onto its edge for dear life. When the sun comes out, I warm up again and turn back into vapor.

Soon I am a cloud again. But I am so tired! Does water always travel so much?

I beg the wind to blow me back to the Oregon coast. The wind blows me back over sea and over land. It blows me up a mountain, through another rainbow, and over the edge of a steep cliff. At last, I rain down onto my beach, and I am a puddle again.

"I never want to shape-shift again!"
I say to the bottle. "Will you turn me
back into a person?"

"You bet!" says the bottle.
"A person is almost all water, too."

BAM! Already, I am me again! It was
fun going all around the world as water,
but it is also good to be a person.

The End

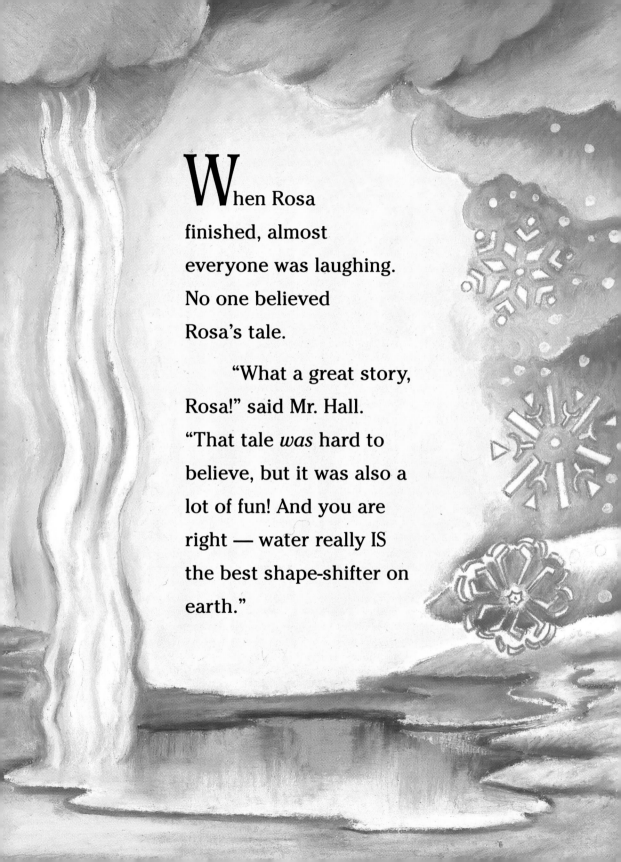

When Rosa finished, almost everyone was laughing. No one believed Rosa's tale.

"What a great story, Rosa!" said Mr. Hall. "That tale *was* hard to believe, but it was also a lot of fun! And you are right — water really IS the best shape-shifter on earth."